T H E
M U N T U
P O E T S
OF CLEVELAND

THE UNITED BLACK ARTISTS OF CLEVELAND
WORKSHOP AND PRESS
and the
FREE LANCE POETS PRESS
Cleveland, Ohio

1 9 6 8

TABLE OF CONTENTS

A man who doesn't wish to remain
in a room

        can't leave it without going to
        its extremes!

                        -- A. Nonymous

INTRODUCTION

Some individual works of art may involve questions of conformity to universally accepted values and definitions. But most "great" art is relatively what a particular group's sense of significance chooses to respect as such. Whether music is or is not liked or what is of worth or significance in it to be studied or not studied or whether poetry is to be written or read or not and what is of worth and significance as poetry - whether there is such a thing as "poetry" or "music" - must be decided by a particular group for itself. This is a true basis of "mind" and freedom. Ethnic groups may less permit themselves to be told what to accept as aesthetic, may less concede special importance to knowing what philosophies, ethics, history or "knowledge" another group organizes as significant except insofar as they have to do with submission for survival. "Knowledge" should not, we believe, continue to be the knowing of others' work before having perceived and decided upon and judged one's own work.

It is possible to create that
which may subsequently be learned
- a much safer and independent
way than being told through
learning what may be created: the
former is the path to invention:
the latter ends in limitations.

                    Russell Atkins

SABABA AKILI

Sababa Akili's poetry has been featured in local newspapers, Cleveland Metro, Community College's <u>Commuter</u> and the <u>Cleveland Call & Post</u> has mentioned his work. He has appeared in Black Art Festivals in Chicago, Detroit and at Central State University. He is on the staff of <u>Uhuru Storm</u>, an Afro-American publication.

BLACK WOMEN, BLACK MEN
(If We Had Been Stronger)

        Beautiful Black Women
        The World's
        Only real Women

        Why are you leaving
        Us
        We now know that if we
                had been
        Stronger- you wouldn't'
        be wearing - wigs - make-up
          mini dresses -
        straightened
          hair

        If we had been
                Stronger
        You wouldn't have to
                imitate miss ann
                you would have been
                freed from slavery
            long ago

        If we had been stronger
        there would have been
                no - whores
                prostitutes
                lesbians
          or bourgeois - Black
        Women.

        Black Women
        Don't leave us

Don't turn away
        from us

We know that if
   you had
been stronger
   we wouldn't
have processed heads

rainbow colored slacks
      and the needle
      to keep us alive

If you had
         been stronger
We wouldn't have
         to imitate
Mr. Charlie we would
have been free
         long ago

If you had been stronger
there would be no
         Pimps
         Slicks
         homosexuals
         or Uncle Tom Black Men

Black Women
      Beautiful Black Women

Our freedom depends on
                YOU
Don't turn your
      Back on boys
         Who are needing to
             become Men

Come To Us
        Black Women
Come Back
        To Black Men

Come Back Beautiful Black Women.

        -- Sababa Akili

RUSSELL ATKINS

is advisor and chairman of the Muntu Workshop. He is founder and co-editor of <u>Free Lance Magazine</u> and his writings have appeared in magazines and anthologies in Europe and America. He is considered to be among the foremost experimentalists in contemporary poetry.

SPYRYTUAL

Oh didn't it   """   """   """
                " "   " "
                " "   " "
                " "   " "
" "   "
 " "   " "   "
        " "   " "

rain
        " "
                " "
        " "   "   "
Oh did
    """   """   n't   ""
        " "   " "

                                it
rain   " "
                " "

                -- Russell Atkins

PERRY DAVIS

is both flute
player and poet.
He is also a
painter of
highly abstract
pictures.

BREAKFAST

And my cornflakes
moaned and giggled
as I poured milk on
them
while the spoon
I held in my hand
pleaded with me not to
take
him away from the fork
for they were
engaged to be wed
the following
Thanksgiving.
The pickle fork was
going to be the
bridesmaid;
the salad fork
the maid of honor
and the finger-bowl
was to perform
the ceremony.
But I, being very
brittle and unkempt,
enjoyed hearing corn
flakes scream
while being beaten
with an engaged spoon.

           -- Perry Davis

B. FELTON

has been active in the
dramatic arts. He has
contributed poems to
Fisk University's
<u>Herald</u>. His work is
presently under
consideration by
Broadside Press of
Detroit and he is
scheduled for readings
the Muntu Workshop at
several colleges
including Smith College.

WITH LOVING ARMS

With loving arms
                    / wrap
bundles of
Hope around me, / squeeze
into my /

/ spirit.

The dawn   /
          / like granules
 of

                            / brown
sugar
Dissolving throughout: /
                    /and with
surety
The unknown will   /
                /surge
forth
                          / as
the known

Draped in wisdom /
                /and
awareness

                    -- B. Felton

MISSISSIPPI

The delta sun cowls its face
As streaming arms of warmth
    carry pulsations of life

Down into rich fertile soil
that
    responds with many gifts -
-

Brown hands reaching for life,
    love and understanding,
under

The watchful gaze of its
helpless friend

                    -- B. Felton

WENDELL HARRIS

teaches at Crispus Attucks Elementary School. Poetry has been his interest since an early age. His poems have been printed in <u>Poetry Parade</u>, <u>Harvest Years</u> and a <u>National Anthology of Poetry</u>. He did community development in the Peace Corps.

"AFTER SISYPHUS"

Sisyphus has given his
children
The stone to roll from dawn to
dusk,
With ears that do not hear and
eyes
        that can not see.

Nothing can lift their sights
from
The ground nor straighten
their
Backs from futile toil.
Flood lights of searching pain
Forever wash the barren
horizon.

In their darkness of confusion
Nothing is more false than
truth
The gods they call upon are
sleeping
        and can not awake.

Poverty makes peace with the
Only existence it knows.
Toil, toil, toil and do not
Die from the weight of the
stone!

For no one can give you
yesterday
Nor promise the tomorrow

This was the message etched
On a face like a forgotten tomb.

Sisyphus had nothing else to
Give his children except the
Burden that dictated his sphere
Nothing can unlock the chain

Except the captured love of
        Pandora's box.

        -- Wendell Harris

JON HALL

has been a faithful
member or the
workshop. He has
read is poems with
the Muntu Workshop
at Community
College's
"Diogenes" Lantern
and CORE's Target
City Festival
during Black Arts
week. His poems are
scheduled to appear
in an anthology
from International
Publishers.

one up,
two back and
four in either direction
left   or   right

we'll skip
     three this
    time but
      we'll get to
    it
by and by
    at that great

"mountain
     in the sky"
  goodfellow perished
     recently:
didn't realize
     his "god-like-ness"--
 now it blasts
     my face in forms
        of mass paraphernalia:
circulars•, magazines, tv, radio,
speeches, sweatshirts, balloons,
and more --
          showing me how to
    be a "good
    Blackman" - DEAD

all hail the
king of
     the
          mountain
                    -- Jon Hall

          half-full, half-empty
too soon, too late, words
     misused, contorted, bent
     out of shape --"hate monger"
"Fire-bomber," "thug," "thief"--
     ascribed to those
  who prophesy
                   fate
be cool, don't wait, get it
together - it's too late
   listen
          to the meaning,
not the words,
   get with the feeling,
  mode, and time --
          let it not run like
water
          thru a sieve-like
mind --
     let your words
be bullets and your mind
     the gun and blast
        when you observe
the whites of
     their eyes

                    -- Jon Hall

NORMAN JORDAN

is director of the Muntu
Workshop of Cleveland.
His plays have been
performed by the San
Diego State College
drama department. His
poems have been accepted
by <u>Soulbook</u>, SNCC's
<u>Afro-American</u> <u>Magazine</u>
and <u>Black Poets Journal</u>.
He is scheduled to
appear in an anthology
edited by LeRoi Jones
and Larry Neal.

THE END CROWD

Dirty Red
told it like
it was
and we pretended
to eat it
up.

HA!
Most of it went right through
our hard heads.

                    -- Norman Jordan

THE SILENT PROPHET

Trane
must
have
died
a
thousand
times
trying
to tell
us
what it
was all
about
but we
were
so
busy
dancin
g
we couldn't hear
his
music.

        -- Norman Jordan

THE ISSUES

We
worship
different Heroes
now.
We stopped
bowing
to Uncle Tom
baseball players
and phony politicians
who drive
long shiny cars
and attend $25 dollar a plate
luncheons
for United Appeal

We now listen
to our bushy-headed
brother
standing on the corner
rapping
out the side
of his mouth
about The Man!

We
worship
different Heroes
now.
Since we
stopped reading the
newspaper
-- Norman Jordan

OMARR MAJIED

is featured editor for the Uhuru Storm a black nationalist newsletter. He has participated in a number or festivals in memory of Malcolm X and devotes his time to "Ask Omarr" a newspaper column.

No no mr Beast
fight your own
fuckin' war
i didn't start it
mr Beast

            your war
don't make
            any sense
mr Beast.

to go
far, far away
from home and kill
those non-whites
for YOU?
mr Beast give me
a gun and i will help you kill
beast people over
here   i ain't
scared when it comes down
to that
that is what you call
a real war

                    -- Omarr Majied

ART NIXON

was born August 24, 1947. He attended Ohio State University for a year and then became an entertainer in various coffeehouses, Night clubs, etc. He has read at Community College's "Diogene s Lantern" and recited his poems for WCLV's Fine Arts Station and for the Canadian Broadcasting Company. His work is scheduled to appear in several publications.

HERE

There is neither night nor day
here, but, a universal
traffic light violated by
a modern mass of
premature grave dwellers
and empty humanity.
A million Mondays
and a lake of coffee
precede the golden years,
and time cards are
hallowed tickets to
enter each day.

And here cannibalistic matrons
of this sad style and life
gambol across fresh cement.
in green dinner jackets
while their hairy behinds
are grinning esoteric versions
of the golden rule
at a flock of weary robots.
The young are weaned
by makeshift mothers (with
legitimate Greek complexes)
and given good reasons
for living by rusty computers.

But the mutants of this zoo
deny the vice of tightening flesh
about the temples and the silent
explosion of nerves that quakes
their illegitimate "piece" of mind,
and sit on top of ideological walls
and
and blissfully swing their feet.

                          -- Art Nixon

RHYTHM OF BLACKNESS

The rhythm of BLACKNESS
labors hot & heavy throughout
the cities,
shaking ominously
even where souls are not,
the rhythm is BLACK and
BLACK is the rhythm:
you here with your body,
even when sweat is dispersed.
The rhythm is thick and
absorbed by the concrete
to make it familiar
with BLACK life of the street.
It bounces off metal,
sinks into flesh,
rubs the night's cloud,
sings in the gutter,
still booming its rhythm --
the BLACKNESS of life.

                    -- Art Nixon

AMIR RASHIDD

is a charter member the workshop. He has read his work at Duke University and University or Pittsburgh. He was a guest reader at the anti-Vietnam war rally in Washington and has been mentioned in several publication's including the Negro Digest. His booklet or poetry The End of Truth's Beginning has just been issued.

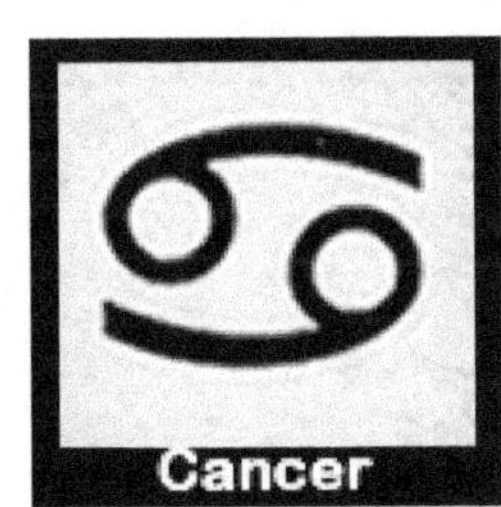

GARGOYLES

How many of their scars are left?

From the wars they lost,
Fighting somewhere beyond their dreams
At the distant end of a stretched
finger,

Reaping the impossible harvest
"-'gro-ing" between the toes of God

Only victories   upon their next
Out-"-'gro-ing" all their deeds

 I sat and wept for them
Only for vained impact across my wet
brow
Wondering why they've lived so long

Hanging in a gray jungle of stones
And I sat dehydrated within the cage
of my frame

"For mercy   for God's sake!"
They plead
                Kill them all
Or maybe I should die

Sitting here crying in this green, drab
Hallway to hell or his house
With brown spots to remind me

                       smelling of blood
And those ancient memories that hide
In drops of poison left
                          in wine flasks
That trim the stairway
That lay cleft between My Ass and the
throne of God
Dying like the invisible seeds of time
Me   screaming in the rain

And you standing staring at the piss
holes in the snow

                    -- Amir Rashidd

MOONING

How sweet was death --!!
as I ran screaming
hoping for someone or something
to free me from this illusion
that haunts the sodden chambers
of my memory.
Hung up in my iniquities,
sleeping with the bride of
disaster,
I cling to something sharp,
sharp,
cutting my fingers.

                    I find myself-
-
I find myself in a forest -
in a forest where all the trees
are gallows
and the dry river bottom a tomb
bulging with those who were
afraid to fight.

The hole in my pellet-stricken
body
forms a suction for the ever
reaping wind
that constantly wrestles for my
heart
knowing I must be free
or become a victim of those
winds;

executed on those same gallows
that grow tilting within my skull
--
picking from their beauty
      the bitter loves of life.

                    -- Amir Rashidd

BILL RUSSELL

has been an editor
of <u>Voice</u>,
a house organ for a
government
program. His poems
have appeared in
<u>Vibrations</u> and <u>Free
Lance</u> <u>Magazine's</u>
Langston Hughes
issue. His work is
being considered by
<u>Cotopaxi</u>, an
international
publication.

A DRY OASIS IN HELL

Spring awakes.
Once again
they come out
to hide morality
in the dust of a bar-room floor.
As darkness falls
over a little oasis
in the middle of hell,
black shadows stand out
against the wood
of a dimly lit bar.
Smoke and funk hang
like a dead cloud
over a graveyard of lost souls.
Some seek out success
in a new world of vocal insult
to a past art called "singin' the
blues."
"oh, baby please don't go!"
some sad song of his love-life
comes from the lips of a simp
as his white, buck-toothed girl
friend
sits by grinning
at a glass of red pluck.

A.D.C. chicks, lye and potato-
head
slicks clap their hands
as the band plays off-key
to a newly made up tune.

A white slick bastard stands by
licking his chops
as two black jaspers
grind their ass
against the bars of a silver
cage.

                -- Bill Russell

Last June
a cat from L.A.
called it a form of rebellion.
But I would just as soon
do something worthwhile
and let this oasis burn
like the rest of this cement
hell.

                -- Bill Russell

CLYDE SHY

is a musician as well as a poet. He has traveled in · Europe with Albert Ayler and has a profound interest in astrology. His appearances include recitals of poetry with music at Cleveland's Ethical Culture Society and at the Institute of Gestalt Therapy, Community College's <u>Lantern</u>, and the Black Arts Festival at Smith College. Canadian Broadcasting Company has taped his work and he is a contributor to Cotopaxi, an international magazine.

I DIG, DUG & DAG

No one saw the dove in his
chest take flight,
Nothing but the third floor
will ever know
where the dove has flown --
where the wind has gone that
once filled his lungs;
That once was his breath;
that once was his moon;
and now his starlight.
Someone (or was it my Venus?)
stamped silence on his lips
and gouged out
his heart with its love and a
broom straw?
Where is old Ben?
He just went away -- I dig.

-- Clyde Shy

STORMY PICNIC

My thoughts tapered to
eye-level and the first
thing
I saw was the past.
I remembered how my past
and I tortured ants
and roaches and how
today
was then. My past
revealed to me how black
was to be. Some old
sounds
banged on my ear drum
and my then pen showed
me
what to write today. I
saw a freak beast saying
how much he enjoyed
digging
in his nose' beating his
meat and vomiting while
sitting in a window
waiting on something
weird
to happen -- something
like L.A. and Detroit.
Nigger bitches who fry their
vibrations and go
whole hog to picnics
to run in the woods and
release their Bar-B-Que
in feelingless "blurtations"

saying fucked up things to a
cracker who eats
the shit up; then back to
town in a '49 Buick sagging on
one side from
the weight of the fat bitch
named "Dot" who wears polka-
dot dresses, who fries
her head and the hogs
in lard: back to town to turn
her nose up
and show her ass to me.

        -- Clyde Shy

www.ingramcontent.com/pod-product-compliance
Lightning Source LLC
Chambersburg PA
CBHW071525030726
47593CB00003B/1405